To The Shepherds
Of The New Millenium

Dr John Dee Jeffries

PUBLISHED by PARABLES
Earthly Stories with a Heavenly Meaning

To The Shepherds Of The New Millenium
Copyright © Dr John Dee Jeffries
Published By Parables

All Rights Reserved. No part of this book may be reproduced or utilized in any form or by any means, electronic or mechanical, including photocopying, recording, or by any information storage and retrieval system, without permission in writing from the author.

Unless otherwise specified Scripture quotations are taken from the authorized version of the King James Bible.

First Edition July, 2017

ISBN 978-1-945698-23-1

Printed in the United States of America

Readers should be aware that Internet Web sites offered as citations and/or sources for further information may have been changed or disappeared between the time this was written and when it is read.

Illustration provided by www.unsplash.com

TO THE SHEPHERDS
OF THE NEW MILLENIUM

DR JOHN DEE JEFFRIES

PUBLISHED by PARABLES
Earthly Stories with a Heavenly Meaning

TO THE SHEPHERDS
OF THE NEW MILLENNIUM
Proverbs 12:17
Dr. John Dee Jeffries

He that speaketh truth sheweth forth righteousness: but a false witness deceit. ~ Proverbs 12:17

The dawn of a new millennium! Shepherds and sheep! And, an old, old story of a Savior come from glory! I have before me an old, worn, well-used Bible from whence the Truth of that story is drawn.

This is my Bible! It is the indisputable, indestructible Word of God! It reveals the Truth about who we are; the Truth about what we have; and the Truth about what we can do as Shepherds of the new millennium!

This is my Bible! It is the inerrant, infallible, Divinely inspired Word of God! Inerrant, because it is pure Truth, without mixture of error. Infallible, because it is the authoritative standard, the Truth about all matters pertaining to faith and practice. Divinely inspired, because it is the very breath, the very Word, the very Truth of God Who cannot lie!

This is my Bible! It tells me the Truth about Who God is and how He is to be experienced.

Hear me, ye Shepherds of the new millennium! The philosophical strength of Christianity resides in its claim to Truth. The theological strength of Christianity resides in its identification of that Truth. Its metaphysical strength resides in its clarification of that Truth while its social strength is found in its call to an experiential relationship with that Truth. (These thoughts were shaped through the influence of Os Guinness, *The GraveDigger File* and *The Dust Of Death*).

Hear me yet again! When those who carry the torch tarnish or taint truth, the Word of God is injured, violence is done to the church, and injustice is done to the common man.

Injury to the Word of God, because we have trivialized the eternal! Violence to the church, because we have diminished the quality of the high standard of the biblical revelation!

Injustice to the common man, because he is led to embrace a brackish truth set forth by one who is disqualified by the

Spirit of God for his failure to fulfill the first, basic, fundamental requirement: an unwavering allegiance to the Truth of God's revelation!

The reputation of Truth, however, is being brought to task. Its value and relevance are being challenged by a veiled counterfeit that parodies itself in a discolored form of reality. The armor of Truth is being substituted with a loose fitting mantle by an alien Captain of Deception. The trumpeting of Truth goes unheard by a Sleeping Giant who has been lulled to slumber by the lullaby of comfort and contentment. The convicting darts of Truth are being masterfully dodged by the psychology of avoidance. The God of Truth is being replaced by the age-old sin of self-enthronement.

There is, indeed, a pitiable shallowness today that is mixing Truth with the murky waters of a haughty and arrogant spirit of self-deification creating an illusion of progress and prosperity. Wisdom, dear brethren, is being shunned for the ignorant darkness of self-sufficiency. The darkness of ignorance is, unfortunately, much more comfortable than the convicting brilliance of Truth, where the demand for self-confrontation leads man to the excruciating realization of his limits; thereby requiring of him a painful search beyond himself for validity! How much more accommodating, I ask, is the broadened canon of tolerance than the canon of righteous restraint! The narrow road that directs man toward peace with God has been broadened into an avenue of tolerance. The Creator God has become a foreign and unwelcomed deity whose Truth has been reduced to a level of contemptuous intrusion.

Indeed, as the post-modern church enters the new millennium Truth is being shaped, reshaped, and shifted devastatingly by the tumultuous winds of a culture in spiritual chaos. In the storm center of swirling spiritual confusion stands the people of God, the people of this post-modern church, and under her ministry umbrella the people entrusted to her care - both inside of and outside of the church.

It is there, within the hearts of these people, if you look carefully, that you will find a cord of love, a cord of longing. It is a cord of love that runs through the heart of every man, that secret place deep within each of us where we thirst and hunger for God. Look deeply, friend, and you will discover that cord of love and longing within your own heart. In The Attributes of God, A. W Tozer writes, "There's a little shrine inside of you, a shrine so far in that nobody can know it but you. There is an innermost part, a deep, deep shrine.". It is there, in this secret place of the heart, that we yearn for and reach out in longing for God.

Augustine wrote, "Our hearts are restless . . . " This restlessness sparks an inward hunger and thirst that leads people, all people, to not only intuitively sense that there is a God but to seek after Him.

Anselm yearned for God and from that innermost part, that deep, deep shrine within he cried through his prayerful pen, "Lord, in hunger I began to seek thee; I beseech thee that I may not cease to hunger for thee. In hunger I have come to thee; let me not go unfed. teach me to seek thee, and reveal thyself to me, when I see thee, for I cannot seek thee, except thou teach me, nor find thee, except thou reveal thyself. Let me seek thee in longing, let me long for thee in seeking; let me find thee in love, and love thee in finding."

I. RESTLESSNESS

A) The Restlessness of the Heathen's Heart

This inward thirst for God, manifested through the pen of Anselm, Augustine and a host of others has often led the heathen, groping in darkness, to sense God. Yet, the heathen has either sensed God as an unnamed Presence or as a vague, incomprehensible Something that created the world, controls the forces of nature, and afflicts pain or heaps reward upon people. Misguided by the revelation of God in nature, the god of the heathen is frequently viewed as a Mysterious Power to be either feared, appeased, or manipulated through various forms of idolatrous worship. The dazzling heathen, whether singing ancient high-pitched hymns around some sacred stone or kicking his knees high in a primitive dance as he circles a sacred well, is affirming with a glad heart what his reason can never comprehend.

In Heretics, G. K. Chesterton wrote, "Once in the world's history men did believe that the stars were dancing to the tune of their temples." Both historical and contemporary cultures verify the propensity of the heathen to seek after and to worship the Unknown. Splashed across the canvass of humanity are sad, colorful images, distinct and different, yet similar, in that they paint the restlessness of the heathen heart.

Listen carefully and you will discover

that idolatry speaks many languages and assumes many disguises. Yet one thing it cannot disguise: the restlessness and yearning of the heart.

A pious Sumerian priest, meditating in an ancient temple of a solar god, trembles as he looks at the brilliance of the sun in an afternoon sky. As he stares intently into the golden glow he silently empties his mind of all thought save that of his solar god. His trembling increases and becomes a violent twitching as he falls to the floor. In a state of ecstasy, he enters into a mystical trance that seemingly transcends both time and space, enabling him to become one with both the universe and the sun god whom he worships.

On a sandy beach of a remote island in the Pacific, a sweating group of tribal leaders dance and chant around the straw image of an airplane, longing for the return of the great silver-winged god of the air who once brought material blessings to their people.

During an annual agricultural liturgy in China, a prince ploughs the first furrow of the new agricultural year in an annual ritual, drawn from the Confucian Classics, leading his people to commune with heaven and worship nature.

The eyes of a Mexican peasant fill with tears as he claps his hand and dances with his daughter during a festival honoring the maize-god.

In a bookstore in Boston, a distraught young lady stands before a revolving rack of books and magazines. In desperation, she chooses a popular paperback that promises to solve her problems by leading her to have a better life through the latent power of crystals.

TO THE SHEPHERD

Every culture has developed and accumulated its own collection of religious tales, sacred myths, and otherworldly legends, which defined the metaphysical context within which its people lived. Think about that context as it relates to the heathen! How many men and women have wondered about the power of a Reality that they sensed existed beyond the natural phenomena of the world? How many, stirred by a trembling religious impulse they could not explain, have looked up in fear when startled by the clap of thunder only to find themselves uttering a silent prayer? Or trembled and called for help from some Supernatural Power when confronted with the sounds hidden in a shadowy forest? While these conceived deities, even when named, are not even a pale reflection of the One True God, that they were and are conceived at all reveals the restless of the human heart.

B) The Restlessness of the Pagan's Heart

History, dear people, also bears witness to the various conceptual tapestries created by pagan cultures and philosophical traditions. Standing in opposition to the heathen these supposedly philosophically enlightened pagans, walking in the dimness of reason and logic, also sense the reality of God. For the pagan, his reason logically tells him that God is greater than nature. Through the unfocused mental lens of the pagan, however, God is often viewed either as the great Undefined or the inexplicable Mystery that spawned and gave birth to the universe. Therefore, with the pagan's brush of logic, God is painted as either the Uncreated Presence, the Ultimate Reality, or the First Cause of all that is. Through the sterile pen of reason, God and His attributes are often bantered about by the pagan in a speculative, metaphysical language that both lacks reverence and produces a joyless religion that appeals to the mind rather than the spirit. These cognitive wanderers, with their minds steeled against the truth, dot the historical landscape from antiquity, surfacing through the ages even into our present age, which is dominated by relativistic New Age philosophic, post-modern thought.

A fourteenth century B.C. Egyptian philosopher-king is caught in political, religious and philosophical controversy as he seeks to establish the New Empire of Egypt that will be guided by a metaphysical god rather than by himself as a deified ruler.

In the city of Tuscany, a twelfth century medieval philosopher fused the three hierarchies of Neo-Platonism to clarify how his followers can move from sensory observation to a mystical vision of the invisible traits of the Uncreated Presence behind the rhythm of the universe.

DR. JOHN DEE JEFFRIES

A young man in a post-modern university is fascinated by the 666 units of the Magical Square of the Sun, in the Western Hermetic tradition, as the calculations seemingly verify that the number 1746 symbolizes the universal spirit, the source of all feminine and masculine processes in nature.

A clairvoyant yoga from India teaches a course at a suburban YMCA in Denver, Colorado, detailing the 101 conduits of the life force in Vedanta, as he carefully instructs his students on the art of arousing and awakening kundalini-shakti, the psychospiritual serpent power that is supposedly located in the lower base of the human spine.

In a sophisticated drawing room of a New Age poetry club in Atlanta, Georgia, a group of young men and women, unintentionally deviating from their assigned metaphysical topic, suddenly find themselves discussing the existence and nature of God.

To each of these a host of historical and contemporary examples could be set forth. Assessing the pagan's philosophical conclusions concerning God, theologian and philosopher Gerhkard Tersteegen, concluded that "[a] comprehended God is no God at all." Thinking of God as He may be conceived of in our imagination is, quite simply, not sufficient. Man, apart from Divine revelation, cannot think correctly about God. The finite cannot comprehend the infinite. Indeed, if the "judgments" of God are "past find out," then how much more so must be God Himself! Augustine understood this. In his Confessions, he wrote, "I wished to meditate upon my God, but I did not know how to think of him." Acknowledging this reality in Psalm 139:6, David said, "Such knowledge is too wonderful for me; it is high, I cannot attain unto it."

The early church father and Christian apologist, John Chrysostom, realized the plight of pagan, speculative thought. He wrote, "For nothing causes such dizziness as human reasoning, all whose words are of earth and which cannot endure to be enlightened from above. Earthly reasons are full of mud, and therefore we need streams from heaven, that when the mud has settled, the clearer portion may rise and mingle with the heavenly lessons." In the midst of this mud stands the pagan; pity his poor soul. Even though the pagan often denies the warmth of a personal God, thereby relegating God to the category of being a thing, rather than a personal Savior, the pagan's speculative thoughts and carefully constructed mental concepts also bear witness to the restlessness of the human heart.

C) The Restlessness of the Fool's Heart

Walking through history, arm-in-arm

with both the heathen and the pagan, is the person described in the Bible as the fool. The psalmist declares that, "The fool hath said in his heart (not in his mind, it should be noted) that there is no God (Psalm 14:1)." Thus, while the mind of the fool intuitively senses that there is a God, his heart denies God's reality because it senses the moral obligation that acknowledgment of God would bring to bear upon itself. Caught in the ever-tightening grip of the sensual part of human nature, with its lusts, cravings, desires and competing drives, the fool is led to deny the reality of God. Sensing the grievous calamity that moral restraint would inflict upon his egocentric lifestyle, the fool, rather than subordinate or subjugate himself to the Divine, casts off any knowledge of the Holy. By denying the reality of God, the fool chooses to cater to the dictates of his lower nature. These disinherited spirits, and the writings that have flowed from their seething and tormented minds, have been present throughout history. Tragically, the prevalence today of these feeble minded characters, with their hearts agitated by their rejection of God, is increasing, even as they confront the ghastly terrors of a culture stained with violence, drug addiction and sexually-transmitted diseases that all stem from their rejection of God.

Many, dear brethren, have found great comfort by telling themselves that God is an imaginary thing; a figment of human imagination and the byproduct of a misguided, collective religious consciousness that lingers from mankind's unenlightened, historic past. "We are beyond that," they tell themselves, "for we have progressed beyond the primitive darkness of ancient myth into the full light of reason." Wandering in a desert of abandoned faith, unbelief has become their illusionary oasis. At the heart of their illusion, they have accepted the idea that man is but living dust lost in the vast expanse of the universe. Hence, the foolish conclusion of one of their most able spokesmen, Mark Twain, who said that "[t]here is no God, no universe, no human race, no life on earth, no heaven, no hell. All an absurd, grotesque dream. Nothing exists but you. And you are nothing but a thought, a lost thought, a useless thought, an orphan thought wandering solitary across everlasting nothingness."

Twain, however, soon discovered that life in this universe, a fallen, hostile environment, violently intrudes into the oasis, shattering the illusion with the darker dimensions of an uncontrollable reality. The intrusions of death, pain, suffering, and human tragedy create the existential moments that produce intuitions and feelings that are inexplicable to the person who denies the reality of God.

Even as a group of drug-addicted college students in a 1960's dormitory celebrate Time Magazine's proclamation that God is dead, they call on God when one of their number is suddenly gripped by a drug-induced seizure.

A sexually promiscuous teenager is relieved as she reads David Hume's discourse denying God and portraying the world as a self-generating machine, a vast self-creating organism. Yet, only a few weeks later, she is overwhelmed by a sense of inexplicable guilt, shame and conviction as she slithers out of the side-door of an abortion clinic.

A government official in Switzerland, overjoyed with the news that a cancerous tumor has been successfully removed from his body, is both overwhelmed and yet confused by a feeling of gratitude to a God that he believes does not exist.

To The Shepherd

During a lecture in a Methodist church in rural Mississippi, the son of a famous atheist, whose mother successfully had prayer removed from the American educational system, describes how the fierceness of his mother's denial actually revealed the reality of the very God whom she denied.

The very fierceness of the fool's denial, the propensity of even fools to call on God during periods of stress, and the fool's dogged sense of guilt and shame when fundamental morality is violated, actually reveal the reality of that which is being denied. As John Baillie writes, in Our Knowledge of God, even those who "deny God with the top of their minds" may believe at the same time "from the bottom of their hearts." Indeed, an eye darkened by either sin or folly is required to refuse to see that there is glory in the heavens and that the firmament is the handiwork of a creative power. The fool's denial of God, however, in a reverse and rather perverse manner, also verifies the restlessness of the human heart.

One of the agonizing problems for the church of the new millennium, friends, is to clarify how she is to speak to a culture that has lost confidence in all absolute or transcendent points of reference. How do you speak to an age that worships at hollow shrines filled with cynicism, sacred doubt and the paradox of spiritual pessimism born of a paganism that rejects God? Indeed, those who have eyes that see and ears that hear will note that the spiritual, metaphysical and philosophical thought forms of our post-modern age are changing.

The traditional threads of thought - the

basic analogies, images, and metaphors that shaped our culture's historic metaphysical identity - are unraveling, losing their credibility and their power to inform.

As the custodian of a truth that is both timeless and transcultural, the church agonizes about how to clothe truth in language, concepts, and thought forms that can communicate to the post-modern mind - a mind that has been disciplined to exclude this very transcendence.

Hear me, brethren! Time is moving on. The dawn of a new millennium is upon us. The old traditionalists are stuck. The young liberals are stumbling. Like the builders of Babel, each is buried under the linguistic rubble of a language that no one understands.

Listen brethren. All is not lost! God's revelation enables a person who receives it to suddenly see what has always been available for every one to see. Faith in this revelation, as Morris H Chapman said recently, allows us "to know the unknowable, see the invisible, think the unthinkable, hear the unheard and plumb the depths of God's revelation." It enables us to peer into, through and beyond the obscurity, qualifying us to speak, not only to our own day, but also of and to the day that is yet to come

II. REVELATION

Revelation: A Divine Intervention

Like a refreshing oasis in the midst of the desert of historical religious experience, we discover a global, transcultural community of people, from every tribe, nation and tongue, who have encountered and experienced God. Their encounter with God came, not through their own initiative, but, instead, by God Himself directly intervening into their lives. This Divine intervention came because God is aware of the catastrophic cause (mankind's fall and the entrance of sin into the world) and the tragic consequences of that cause that have made it impossible for people to gain a true knowledge of His nature and being.

God knows that when people look at the universe, their view of the Mystery that brought it into existence cannot be more than a glimpse. Even then, this glimpse may be delusive. While it is true that "since the beginning of the world the invisible attributes of God, for example, His eternal Power and Divinity, have been plainly discernible through things which He has made and which are commonly seen and known…" (Romans 1:20 Phillips translation), the plight of the heathen, the pagan and the fool necessitated Divine intervention. Because the restlessness of the human heart cannot refrain from seeking an explanation of the universe, God has given a revelation of Himself that is greater than that contained in nature. This revelation reveals that God seeks to calm the restlessness of the heart and that He will not allow the reality of Who He is or how people can enter into a relationship with Him to be obscured by either nature, the heathen, the pagan or the fool.

That fiery prophet who ascended Mt. Horeb recorded the earliest written revelation of God's intervention. God, stepping from eternity into time, as His Own Interpreter, made Himself known to this prophet. It was this prophet who recorded for posterity the initial revelation of Who God is and how He is to be experienced. The vehicle whereby He made this revelation known is preserved from antiquity in what today is called the Bible.

Yet, in this post-modern age the volcano has blown and the rich, life-giving landscape of the biblical understanding of Who God is and how He is experienced has been covered in the gray ash of contemporary thought that extinguishes rather than sustains.

"For many," writes John Piper in Desiring God, "the childlike wonder and awe have died. The scenery and poetry and music of the majesty of God have dried up like a forgotten peach at the back of the refrigerator."

As sparks flew upward, Christian prophets like Tozer, Lewis, Phillips and others, were flung as burning embers across the theological landscape of the last century. They smoldered, then ignited, with the flame of their torches feeding on the unseen, setting the very air on fire, lighting the way, seeking to astonish and awaken God's church through their prophetic pens. Like the prophets of old, these refugees from yesterday wore a halo of sanctity, had long memories and a fierce loyalty to Truth; qualities that linger, indelibly stamped on our memories and imaginations. They stood in a howling theological wilderness like solitary prophets, weeping over a world becoming more and more empty of God.

Who is this God?

Attempting to describe God is like trying to paint a portrait of someone you have never seen. Each person, however, has an inward portrait of God that is painted, not with brush and paint, but with thoughts and words, on the canvas of their mind. These inward portraits of God help us develop an understanding of Who God is and how we can relate to Him. Each word or thought is like a dab of paint adding color to our portrait of God.

History reveals, unfortunately, that some people have developed terribly distorted portraits of God. Paul wrote about these people, describing them as people who "think up silly ideas of what

God was like and what he wanted them to do and their foolish minds became dark and confused" (Romans 1:21 Living Bible).

God, as already stated, was not willing to allow the reality of Who He is or how He is to be experienced to be obscured by either nature, the heathen, the pagan or the fool. Through His revelation, He has made Himself known. Because the Bible is God's revelation of Himself to man, it is critical that we allow the Bible to be what the Christian church has always known it to be, holy truth that is wholly true; Truth without mixture of error for its matter because the primary matter to which the Bible speaks is God Himself.

Think of it! God's revelation, the Bible, records that the magnificent, omnipotent, eternally self-existent One, Who was before there was a beginning, or time, or space, or anything, has chosen to make

Himself known.

This God, Who fills all things, yet is contained by none, Who exists within eternity, yet is greater than eternity, has stepped from eternity into time. His intention? To reveal, not just His characteristics, qualities or attributes, but His identity -- Who He is -- and how we can relate to Him. His revelation? The astounding reality that He is One, a Singular Being, yet a union of three persons -- Father, Son and Holy Spirit -- and that He, as Father, invites His children, the Son's disciples, through the intimate presence of the Holy Spirit in their lives, to share in and experience the profound intimacy of Their union.

To The Shepherd

A Duel Dilemma

Knowing God, therefore, is not only a relationship to be explained by writing, reading or preaching appropriate statements about Him, but a relationship to be experienced and enjoyed by all believers as children of God. Herein, however, lies an ongoing, duel dilemma for the post-modern church of the new millennium, a tragedy that has been mourned by stalwart men of God throughout the twentieth century.

With the dawn of the new millennium, the traditional understanding of Who God is and the historic understanding of how He is experienced are being shaped, reshaped, and shifted devastatingly by tumultuous theological and philosophical winds as truth is cast about in spiritual chaos.

In the storm center of swirling spiritual confusion stands the post-modern church and, under her umbrella, the people who will shape both the ontological and existential truth for the next generation. With the destructive uprooting of once carefully sown biblical understandings that were planted by pious hands, the church of the new millennium is confronted with the necessity of defining and clarifying the historic, revealed identity of the God of Scripture and the truth of how He is experienced.

Kierkegaard wrote, "In every way it has come to this, that what one now calls Christianity is precisely what Christ came to abolish."

To The Shepherd

In Heretics, Chesterton wrote, "There is a collapse of the intellect as unmistakable as a falling house," It is that collapse, dear brethren, that has produced this ongoing, duel dilemma for the post-modern church at the dawn of this new millennium.

The First Horn of the Dilemma

The first horn of this dual dilemma concerns the image of God, or the understanding of Who God is, held by many within the church of the new millennium. The tragedy of the post-modern image of God held by today's church is that it is so base, so inferior, so vulgar, so ignoble, so tragically flawed, when held in comparison to the biblical revelation. A.W. Tozer, J.I. Packer, J.B. Phillips, C.S. Lewis, and a host of other modern prophets, have all noted that the greatness of God, His grandeur, His very splendor, majesty and magnificence have all been debased. With one voice they have mourned, weeping through their pens and their pulpits. In Knowing God J.I. Packer sadly stated that "false ideas have grown up surrounding God like a hedge of thorns, hiding Who He is from view, and it is no small task cutting through this tangle of mental undergrowth." Tozer, overwhelmed by the low estimate of God held by the modern church added that "the Church has surrendered her once lofty concept of God and has substituted for it one so low, so ignoble, as to be utterly unworthy of thinking, worshipping men."

While it is true that the official statements, documents and decrees by the major institutions of the modern and post-modern church are cloaked in language that is stridently consistent with the biblical revelation, question the average man in the pew concerning his understanding of Who God is and ask probing questions to explore his understanding and the dilemma is verified.

To The Shepherd

In The Screw Tape Letters, C. S. Lewis writes, "The average contemporary man has been accustomed, ever since he was a boy to having half a dozen incompatible philosophies dancing about together in his head."

Worse still, listen to the more than typical seeker-friendly, psycho-babble of the average pulpiteer today and we will see why the future will require more of God's church than the past has required. In Search of Certainty, John Guest writes, "Instead of the ad gloriam of God, we have the ad nauseam of man." In The Gravedigger File, Os Guiness adds that we have "exchanged the 'Holy of Holies' for the 'vanity of vanities.'" In Your God Is Too Small, J.B. Phillips was wounded and grieved by the low estimate that many Christians have concerning God. He saw the sad struggles and the great silent collapse of a faithful yet exhausted clergy as they sought to penetrate the seemingly invincible cloud of ignorance produced by the derelict state of the Christian mind. Phillips, described by his wife as "a wounded healer," raised his pen like a sword against the enormous, unspoken disappointment of the intellectual amputation that produced that collapse. The great English preacher, Charles Hadden Spurgeon, as he and a few good men stood and fought together, yet alone, in the howling wilderness to stem the tide in his generation noted that "The strong are not always vigorous, the wise not always ready, the brave not always courageous and the joyous not always happy."

Someone once said that "no possible arrangement of bad eggs can ever make a good omelet." It is the bad eggs arranged by the metaphysical magicians of the last generation that have spawned this duel dilemma.

In Ashamed of the Gospel, John Mac Arthur correctly assessed the situation, "For most of the past century, evangelical theology has bowed at the shrine of academia, attempting to assimilate secular theology, philosophy, politics, psychology, moral relativism, evolutionary theory, and every other academic fad. Finding those things incompatible with the Bible and the simplicity of the gospel, Christians have too often been willing to twist and shape divine truth to make it fit."

In The Gravedigger File, Os Guiness writes, "The church, is like a person paralyzed from the neck down - quite insensible to the further damage being inflicted on her."

The Second Horn of the Dilemma

Flowing from the pitiable, tattered, post-modern image of God is the second horn of the present day dilemma, the experience of God. A basic distinction between Christianity and other religions is that Christianity goes beyond statements explaining Who God is and offers believers the experience of God Himself. Christianity is greater than an ideology, certainly greater than propositional truth, and goes beyond being a simple code of ethics, a series of moralistic rules, or even principles for governing and guiding one's life. Through Christianity we not only know about God, thereby gaining an understanding of Who He is, but we also come to understand how we can enter into a relationship with Him whereby we experience God in every aspect and area of our lives. Indeed, as stated earlier, God, as Father, invites His children, the Son's disciples, through the intimate presence of the Holy Spirit in their lives, to share in and experience the profound intimacy of Their union. Today, the intimacy of personal experience with God has been affected and infected in at least two ways. For some, the reality of personal experience with God has been replaced with the aforementioned code of ethics, or moralistic rules, or principles to govern and guide one's life. For others, this personal experience with God has been translated into a leisurely quasi-spiritual walk through life -- a vague, ambiguous, "touchy-feely" kind of walk, guided by feelings, impulses and impressions rather than the Spirit of God.

With the dawn of the new millennium, brethren, the dual-dilemma of the post-modern church has reached a crisis point that is both deep and profound, calling for intensive institutional introspection and sober individual reflection. Understand that the two horns of this dilemma are intertwined, having a similar relationship one to the other, in that each informs and shapes the other. Whether she is conscious of it or not, the post-modern church at its very heart is dealing with a genuine crisis in the realm of truth. It is a crisis of truth both ontologically, that is, concerning Who God is, His nature and being, and existentially, that is, in the realm of the experience of God. This crisis has profound consequences.

The Revelation Of History

Both sacred and secular history reveal that man's experience of God has been most sincere and most prolific during those periods when instruction concerning the nature of God and His truth have been consistent with the biblical revelation and clearly established in the hearts and minds of those who are under the ministry umbrella of the church. The opposite has occurred when the life blood of God's church, God's revelation of Who He is and how He is experienced, has been forced to flow through a diseased, sacrilegious heart.

Nietzsche, an atheistic philosopher, stood like a king with his cold face and, ironically, raised the right question, "Who is wise enough for this moment in history?" Nietzsche, history records, because he found no answer, went insane and eventually died by his own hand. The post-modern church, however, must be wise enough and spiritual enough to ask the questions demanded of this moment in history (Who is God? And, How is He experienced?) and courageous enough to provide biblical answers that are consistent with God's revelation. Like Nietzsche, if the Western church were to die, ("Inconceivable!" you say?), she will die of her own hand. Like Christ, the Western church will be wounded in the house of her friends.

Delusional Thinking

Some, dear brethren, may foolishly view the present trauma of tainted ontological and existential truth as a singular and tragic phenomenon, as a historical accident unique to these times, hopefully, not to be repeated. This is delusional thinking. This is passivity. Those who think this way ignore history. They sigh a passive sigh of spiritual relief, falsely believing that the problem will resolve itself, not seeing the imminent defeat inherent in the neglect of intensive institutional and individual introspection, solitude, serious thought and communion with God. Ignorance, tolerance and passivity is their canon, a canon that will facilitate the establishment of the culture of the Golden Calf, totally permeated by false images of God and dominated by mass episodes of esoteric experiences mingled with the occult and fantasy. The poet Melville's "black flower" -- a noxious weed of condemnation -- may yet "blossom as it may" -- casting a dark, dismal shadow over the church of the new millennium.

Hear me yet again, brethren, hear me! Christianity's philosophical strength resides in its claim to Truth. Its theological strength resides in its identification of that Truth. Its metaphysical strength resides in the clarification of that Truth while its social strength is found in its call to existential relationship with that Truth. And, the first casualty to fall in a spiritual war is the church's understanding of Truth!

Churchill was right when he said, "The truth is incontrovertible, malice may attack it, ignorance may deride it, but in the end; there it is." And the caution of Richard of St. Victor in Gratia contempiationis needs heeding today, "I hold all truth in suspicion which the authority of the Scripture does not confirm." Even Aristotle understood the value of Truth, when he said, "Dear is Plato, but dearer still is truth."

Shaping The Future

The effectiveness of the post-modern church in answering these relevant questions (Who is God and How is He experienced) and in dealing with the issues that flow from the answers to these questions, will not only reveal the future, but shape, not just the early years of this new millennium, but the decades and possibly the centuries that follow. Clearly, friends, any ineffectiveness by the post-modern church will leave behind a terrible trail of wounded individuals, institutions and cultures. What the post-modern church does in relation to this duel dilemma, and how it does what it does as it seeks to answer the relevant questions and deal with these critical issues, will either add to or diminish her respect and spiritual influence on her members, in particular, and on culture in general. A foolhardy approach will create greater weakness and deterioration within the Western church and Western culture. This is not the time, brethren, for spiritual gridlock, distractions or diversions, for they will bring about greater loss of credibility. Although the post-modern church may fulfill its institutional responsibilities by developing and attempting to implement discipleship and evangelistic strategies, she will have great difficulty in raising a sufficient army of evangelistic disciples necessary to implement those strategies. The post-modern church will experience even greater difficulties in dealing with other issues relative to the spiritual welfare of the church and culture until the crisis of Who God is and how He is experienced is effectively resolved. The wake left by an ineffective process will be horribly destructive and greatly hinder the development of an appropriate spiritual infrastructure to minister effectively in the new millennium.

In the midst of this duel dilemma that has brought about the post-modern crisis, the devil's basic, fundamental strategy is actually rather simplistic, yet more devious in its intent as the new millennium unfolds. It is the same strategy that began in Eden, the discoloring of Truth. This same strategy continues into the new millennium with a relentless ferocity. It is a strategy perpetrated in the very pit of hell. The strategy's goal? To divest the biblical documents, the revelatory events that spring from those documents, and the Christian truth within those events, of their original intent. And the purpose of this strategy? To accomplish the integration of a global multi-religious culture for the ultimate purpose of undermining the freedoms of the Western culture in general and the historical facts of Western Christianity in particular. The devil strategizes that a culture that is divested of its historical traditions and the freedoms that are generated by those traditions will feel no obligatory debt to its ancestral heritage and, as a consequence, become complacent enough to be ideologically reconstructed. Through this ideological reconstruction of Western culture, all that will remain within the culture is a miniaturized, shadow type of privatized Christian faith diluted by religious pluralism and a faint, depleted Christian memory. With the constriction of faith and the depletion of Christian memory the church of the new millennium will lack both influence and power. A new reconstituted culture will then rise; the culture of the Golden Calf, totally permeated by false images of god and dominated by mass episodes of esoteric experiences mingled with the occult and fantasy.

Renewal And Reformation

History reveals that the church has been through such problems in the past, from false theologies to false Christologies, with each leaving spiritual damage to large portions of the church and the culture where the church struggled with these issues. And yet, the church has miraculously survived, and become stronger with each challenge, because God has blessed His church, throughout history, with the prophetic leadership necessary to provide the light, guide the church and bind the wounded. History also reveals, brethren, that wherever and whenever the church, under the leadership of competent, committed leaders, has unapologetically, unashamedly and unhesitatingly manifested a fierce determination to cling to biblical truth, the Holy Spirit of God has given His blessings. The biblical words of renewal and reformation have been repeated again and again through the long history of the church during times of ontological and existential crisis, especially in the midst of missed opportunities, always calling the church to return to the genius of our spiritual forefathers, the recipients of Divine revelation. In The Gravedigger File, Os Guiness writes, "History verifies, that, like an eternal jack-in-the-box, Christian truth will always spring back." The final vote is not yet in, nor is the long, arduous battle for ontological and existential truth concluded. In A Faith For Tough Times, Harry Emerson Fosdick wrote, "Granted the glaring faults of the church, the living gospel is too much alive for any church's failures to utterly deaden it." With the present demise of Christian ideas, ideologies, philosophies and institutions, however, the post-modern church cannot afford, dear brethren, another series of missed opportunities.

DR. JOHN DEE JEFFRIES

A Caution And A Challenge For The Post-Modern Church

We must know, brethren, this is not the first time in the church's history, nor will it be the last, that the church must contend for ontological and existential truth. This is not just a passing crisis. It is a cumulative reflection of the unresolved, deeper theological, philosophical and institutional problems of the last century of the previous millennium that the church cannot easily set aside.

For the two horns of this duel dilemma to be dealt with effectively, the institutional pursuit of truth must prevail over the passion for action. Institutional leaders, clergymen and laity of the post-modern church must relearn how to yield and allow the Spirit of God to use them to guard the attitudes, guide the actions, and govern the activities of the post-modern church. To be effective, leadership within the post-modern church must also decide not to compromise the integrity of the biblical revelation. Prophetic leadership must rise above the confused message of post-modern ideologies, philosophies and theologies, no matter how popular they might be, and do what is right for the post-modern church -- lead it to firmly rest on biblically-based ontological and existential truth.

This is not going to be easy. It should also not be interpreted as a call to historic retrogression where the practice of abused power has been so prevalent. Much of the historic ecclesiastical and institutional power of the past few centuries has been built on the ruins of institutions and at the cost of theological careers and reputations. Time and again the process of resolving serious theological problems became part of an ugly pattern of political life within God's church. The blood drawn from sharp double-edged theo-political swords, by combative but allied armies fighting on the same side, yet against one another, has scarred sacred history, leaving a marred trail of serious scandals, internal investigations, and attack policies. This type of process, in a very real sense, is part of that dark side of church life that has regrettably surfaced throughout much of church history. Even though the wheel of history continues to turn in strange ways, such a resurrection of errant, arrogant, narcissistic, theo-political power at this critical hour must be avoided. Will it now end? Or will those in positions of power say the right words but fail to end the trench warfare. The post-modern church must be wise enough to avoid the temptation of spiritual narcissism and institutional arrogance in the process of resolving the duel dilemma of Who God is and how He is experienced. Her theo-political swords must be beaten into plowshares. The lion must lie with the lamb by resisting the temptation toward any type of violent historic retrogressions. The task of the post-modern church is to work together in cooperation with those who embrace biblical revelation. The common, cooperative goal? The re-establishment of biblical truth concerning Who God is and how He is experienced.

Assessing The Future

In The Death of Christian Culture, John Senior writes, "It is said that Christianity, if it is to survive, must face the modern world, must come to terms with the way things are in the sense of the current drift of things. It is just the other way around: If we are to survive, we must face Christianity . . . Christianity, like everything else when it succeeds, grows fat, falters, almost fails until -- unlike other things -- it gets hold of itself again because Christ promised to stay with it until the end . . . For those who border on despair, especially now, it is essential to remember that the Church has never looked so much like Christ as when she was *broken and betrayed from within.*" (Italics added).

The way the wind is blowing as the post-modern church enters the early years of a new millennium is, indeed, troubling. But, now is neither a time for panic nor dire conclusions. Those who are cynical, skeptical or pessimistic about the future of God's church are usually cynical, skeptical or pessimistic about the biblical revelation and about God's ability to use them to change the current of unfolding history. They defend the merits of the desert while preaching an illusive, never-to-be-reached promised land.

There are two devices in literature that should be mentioned at this juncture. One device, known as the Black Moment, carries the intrigue of an unfolding drama to a point of despair where all seems lost -- just before the final deliverance. The second literary device, the White Moment, brings the players within the drama (and the reader, too, it might be added) to a crescendo of joy, hope and adulation -- just before the intrusion of disaster, defeat and despair.

Science fiction writer Arthur C. Clarke wrote: "We are living at a time when history is holding its breath and the present is detaching itself from the past like an iceberg that has broken away from its moorings to sail across the boundless ocean."

Jesus related," The gates of hell shall not prevail" (Matthew 16:18). Chesterton noted, "At least five times, the Faith has to all appearances gone to the dogs. In each of these five cases, it was the dog that died."

As we look, with the eyes of the Spirit, at the post-modern church and compare it with the fresh revelation of the Word of God, one global theme immediately grips our attention. The post-modern church is caught in the midst of a violent spiritual conflict. God's Word very clearly enunciates the magnitude of this conflict, utilizing glowing terms and graphic language. The Scripture describes a global, universal, spiritual war between the Kingdom of God, His Kingdom of Light and that of the Adversary and his kingdom of darkness! Further, the New Testament indicates that as we approach the "latter days" certain "perilous times" would unfold, escalating, increasing, and intensifying as the day of Christ approaches (1 Timothy 3:1). In the original language of Scripture the word for "perilous times" literally means "times filled with pressure" that cause "great perplexity, consternation, and fear" to rise up within the hearts and minds of people. The vivid imagery of the word "perilous" portrays great waves of humanity, including those within the church, as being driven to and fro by spiritual pressures, spiritual entities and spiritual forces operative in the midst of the conflict.

DR. JOHN DEE JEFFRIES

The Often Unseen, Unfolding Patterns Within Culture

The very chaos of contemporary existence within Western culture reveals that the post-modern church is at a pivotal point, for culture at its very heart is religion externalized. Although logical explanations detailing and defining sociological causes that have created the current circumstance can be presented, up to a point, the actual seeing of the invisible, unfolding pattern within the present circumstance is not sequential, and therefore is not easily seen. As these unfolding, invisible patterns suddenly emerge to the surface, the essence of what has been and what is occurring is suddenly grasped. Many otherwise inexplicable events and trends that have been and are continuing to transpire within the spiritual environment of the post-modern church and Western culture are beginning to fall into place.

Man's most crucial learning tool is in making mental connections. The essence of human intelligence is to forge mental links; to go beyond the superficiality of the given; to see patterns, relationships, and context. At this present juncture in history, the post-modern church is being roused by the trumpet of alarm through an additional consequence of this ontological and existential crisis, the sophisticated negation of Christian morality. While it is true that the church must be zealously innovative in discerning ways to clarify and weave moral values into the fiber of the people entrusted to her care, it is equally true, and even more expeditious, that she deal with the root of the problem. Because the church has surrendered her distinctive identity, an identity based on the biblical image of God, her members have become secularized, spiritually schizophrenic, and as a consequence, morally and ethically lobotomized. Studies indicate that the derelict state of the Christ mind concerning Who God is and how He is experienced have produced a post-modern believer that is spiritually, morally and ethically formless, like water constantly reshaping itself to its surroundings. Large portions of the church of the new millennium, however, have failed to link the present moral crisis to the ontological crisis of Who God is and the existential crisis concerning how He is experienced. The mental connection simply has not been made. The pattern has not been seen. The mental link has not been forged. Instead, it remains broken. The angels of heaven weep as large portions of the post-modern church continue hacking at the branches of the sophisticated negation of Christian morality while the root cause, the diminishing sense of the holiness of God, is given little if any consideration.

Seeing the reality of what is unfolding and why it is unfolding within the postmodern church and Western culture might be compared to the childhood challenge of discovering the "hidden pictures" in children's magazines. When I was a boy these "hidden picture" sketches were very popular. A pen and ink sketch was presented to the reader, perhaps of a cloud-covered mountain surrounded by tall trees and a calm lake. Beneath the cleverly drawn sketch were instructions challenging the reader to examine the sketch more closely -- to search for certain things that no rational mind would have reason to believe were in the sketch -- "hidden pictures." Camouflaged within the sketch were objects. The mountain hid a hamburger. A tree branch was actually a toothbrush. The lines around the lake formed a baseball bat. Hidden images, on closer inspection, would suddenly emerge. The reader could not be talked into seeing these "hidden pictures" -- they had to be seen. They were either seen or they were not. That was the challenge of the game: to see that which was not readily seen, that which no one expected to see. Once the "hidden pictures" were seen, however, they became plainly visible whenever the sketch was viewed.

Here, plainly stated, is the "hidden picture." At this present juncture in history the post-modern church is imprisoned by fallacious images of God and how He is experienced, sketches that have been drawn by the maverick theologians and philosophers who inhabited the last few centuries of the prior millennium. The post-modern church has not fallen into this crisis because truth has failed. She is where she is because she failed to see the fallacious "hidden pictures" imbedded within the theological and philosophical sketches that have dominated her recent history.

DR. JOHN DEE JEFFRIES

To The Prophets of the New Millennium

Only God and history, dear brethren, as I shared earlier, will ultimately verify the true color of this moment in history (White Moment? Black Moment?) and the distant shore to which this moment is taking us. However, beneath the unfolding drama of this post-modern crisis, God has His torchbearers, the prophets of the new millennium. I salute you, my brothers. It is to you and for you that I speak. You are the strong nails that hold the church together. You are an assorted group, often ministering in obscurity, smoldering. Like Tozer, Packer, Phillips,

Lewis, and a host of men of renown from the previous generation, you too will spark, sending bursts of light streaming through the post-modern church as the new millennium unfolds. With one voice, you and your fellows, like refugees from the past, will mourn and weep through your pens and pulpits, seeking to astonish and awaken God's church. Indeed, you see what a certain poet once saw -- that the wall on which the ancient prophets wrote is cracking at the seams. Some of you are old. Some are young. Even now you are shaping the future of the post-modern church in significant ways. You are turning away from the fallacious philosophical and pseudo-theological confusion of the recent past. You seek and long for, not a modern God made in the image of man, but the ancient God of Scripture, the God of Abraham, Isaac and Jacob, the God and Father revealed through the Son and confirmed in your hearts by the Spirit. However diverse your personalities and your stations in life, each of you agree on one very important point: the post-modern church of the new millennium has arrived at a major intersection, a Cross-road, if you will, and must return to the biblical revelation concerning ontological and existential truth.

To you whom God is raising up: Cherish your small victories. Treasure them, for collectively they will produce the long-awaited awakening. Remember, Providence appears in many guises. We often entertain angels unawares. Remember too that time is redemptive and valuable; circumstance is providential, filled with Christ and His leading. Experience is not what happens to you but what you do with what happens to you. Accept the reality that dissolution and pain are but necessary stages inherent in the process of recovery. Receive encouragement through whom God provides and know with certainty that the deeper the dark night of despair and the more that dissolution creeps around the edge of the present circumstance, the brighter the light from God that beckons you to not trivialize the Eternal.

In Orthodoxy, historian G. K. Chesterton wrote "Do not, I beseech you, be troubled about the increase of forces already in dissolution. You have mistaken the hour of the night: it is already morning."

> The noble army
> of the martyrs praise thee
>
> TE DEUM

DR. JOHN DEE JEFFRIES

A Psalm of The Apocalypse
That Which Was, Which Is, And Is Yet To Come

May God Open Your Eyes
That You May See His Deeds, and
Your Ears That You May Hear His Voice

John the Younger, Son of Cosmas,
Son of John from the Isle of Greece

From *The Last Martyr*
Dr. John Dee Jeffries

In the Candle – in the darkness
A slender flame leaps – in solitude.
Its flame. Its flame.
With fiery mouth thunders.
Eschatos. Eschatos.
It Hungers. Hungers.
Its tongue, a flame, hungers.
Eschatos. Eschatos.
Shiv`a

TO THE SHEPHERD

Jezreel. Jezreel.
Stained with Blood. Graves, Open,
Bone-Filled.
Widen their jaws.
A Gathering of Armies. Falling Stars.
Merj ibn-'Amir, the Plain of Megiddo.
War Men at the End of Time
Broken Seals. An Ancient Rhyme.
The Wound of Death. Blood, Bridle Deep.
Infidels Salute. Angels Weep.
TE DEUM.

Six, Imperfection, the Number of Man
Six thrice, Woe unto the Earth, the Beast
In the Latter Day, his Feast –
Six, Imperfection, the Number of Man
War Man at the End of Time
Zarathustra
An Image – A Symbol -- Who will understand?
Six thrice, the Number, the Beast, a Man
Shiv`a.

DR. JOHN DEE JEFFRIES

Zarathustra
A Dark Seed Blossoms
Flowers, Black, Three in Number, Stand Tall
Shadows, Bleak, a Terrible Fall.
Kyrie Boethei. Lord Help.
Lord Help Us All.
Trisagion – Holy, Holy, Holy
Thrice Holy -- Agios O Theos –
Tersanctus.
TE DEUM.

Three. Three. Shaped by the Pen.
Recurrence. Recurring, Again and Again.
Philosophers Three – All Agree
What Ill Hath Befallen Thee
Camus' Foul Sons, Foul Sons Thou Art
Who are, will be, yet are not --
A Devious Plot.
He Who Has Eyes, See.
Unholy Trinity. – Unholy Three.
Avel.

To The Shepherd

Seven, the Number of Perfection
And of Weeks
Daniel saw Seventy, of Years
One Disappears, Cut Off – Eternal Tears
Yet, Once More, In the Holy Land
The Unholy Zarathustra
He Will Stand
Seven, Perfection. Six thrice, a Man.
Keriah.

One Week Remains, Singular. Alone.
Earth's Final Judgment –
The Great White Throne
In the Candle – in the darkness
A slender flame leaps – in solitude.
Like a Sheep led to Slaughter
He Died for His Own
One Remains, Singular. Alone.
Shiv`a. Keriah. Avel. Keriah. Shiv`a.

Dr. John Dee Jeffries

One remains
Only One, One Week of Years
The Lamb, The Lion -- Final Tears
Jacob's Time of Trouble.
It now appears.
A labyrinth leads the way,
But not in the light of day.
The time is fulfilled.
Final Trump.
Shiv`a.

The horsemen. The horsemen.
Four in number.
Apocalypse. Apocalypse.
Do not slumber.
Burning Winds. Twisted Land.
Waters Rise and Rage.
Eschatos. Eschatos.
The Lion. The Lamb. The Cage.
Avel

To The Shepherd

Seven Cities Rise, Seven Cities Fall
One, On Seven Hills -- The Leader of All
Like A Rope Stretched O'er the Abyss
Unholy Pope. Something Amis.
Secular City, Once Sacred, Sterile,
Stained Within
Antiochus. That Swine.
Flee Babylon, the Harlot, the Whore
The Closed Door.
Avel.

The Sound of Weeping
The Feel of Fear,
Jacob's Day of Trouble, Drawing Near
Nations Rejoice,
Blinded, No Choice
The Righteous, Few,
Beat The Breast, Bow The Head
Find A Pew
Shiv`a.

DR. JOHN DEE JEFFRIES

Seven Final Thunders
The Nations, They Shudder, They Cry
Mountains fall on us, lest we die
Seven Heads Turn, Seven Crowns Fall
Seven Kings Weep – Earth, Final Call
Can these bones live?
God's Scepter Shall Bless.
1000 years. A Holy Rest.
Selah.

Zarathustra. Zarathustra.
Overman, Underman, An Unholy Jeer.
A Divine Funeral,
The Procession Draws Near
The Sound of Weeping
Sharia law(less) Unholy Dread
Who Will Bow The Head
God Is Dead
Shiv`a. Keriah. Avel. Keriah. Shiv`a.

TO THE SHEPHERD

God Is Dead. God Is Dead.
Thus Spake Zarathustra –
His scandalous tongue seduces many
The Nations Shout with Glee
An Unholy Harmony
God Is Dead.
Say The Unholy Three
God Is Dead. God Is Dead.
Templum aedificavit – Build A Temple
TE DEUM.

Fiery Trial. Fiery Trial. A Hard Example.
Sacred Blood through Flames Trample.
Learn Patience Beneath their Altar
As they sing Retribution's Psalter
How long, O Lord,
How long shall we wait?
The last living Martyr at Menorah's Gate
His death will soon pass
The last shall be first and the first last
Shiv`a.

DR. JOHN DEE JEFFRIES

See -- The Just Man –
Struggling For Breath
Running to Certain Death
He, a Martyr, the Last, Runs, Yet Not Alone
Nor for sin does he Atone -- But for Fear
It crawls down his cheek, a tear
At his Death, Two Olive Trees, They Appear.
End Time Prophets. Slain. The Second Woe.
The first shall be last and the last first
Shiv`a.

Strong Nails, God's Men,
Refugees From The Past
Hold the Church Together, Stand, Steadfast
Through Pen, Through Pulpit
Astonish. Awaken. Arouse.
Knowing therefore the terror of the Lord
Soon Judgment Will Fall
The Wall, The Wall
On Which Ancient Prophets Wrote
Cracking at the Seams
Hell's Final Stroke

To The Shepherd

The Trump, The Trump
The Last, The Final Call
Even So, Come Quickly, Lord Jesus,
Come, Come for All
Pause. Praise.
His Anthem Raise.
Selah.

DR. JOHN DEE JEFFRIES

TO THE SHEPHERD

Pathways To The Past

Each volume stands alone as an Individual Book
Each volume stands together with others
to enhance the value of your collection

Build your Personal, Pastoral or Church Library
Pathways To The Past contains an ever-expanding
list of Christendom's most influential authors

Augustine of Hippo
Athanasius
E. M. Bounds
John Bunyan
Brother Lawrence
Jessie Penn-Lewis
Bernard of Clairvaux
Andrew Murray
Watchman Nee
Arthur W. Pink
Hannah Whitall Smith
R. A. Torrey
A. W. Tozer
Jean-Pierre de Caussade
And many, many more.

DR. JOHN DEE JEFFRIES

Contact Information

Published By Parables
We Publish Christian Books -- FREE
Dr. John Dee Jeffries
CEO/Acquisitions Editor
Email: fbc.chalmette@gmail.com
www.Published By Parables.com

At this writing John has authored six books:
The Last Martyr
When I Can't Find God
Hip. Hip. Hallelujah 1, 2 & 3
To The Shepherds Of The New Millenium

Books *Published By Parables*
Are available through Amazon,
Barnes and Noble, Books-A-Million,
and wherever fine Christian books are sold.

TO THE SHEPHERD

DR. JOHN DEE JEFFRIES

www.ingramcontent.com/pod-product-compliance
Lightning Source LLC
Chambersburg PA
CBHW071750080526
44588CB00013B/2209